2012

dIREsTRAITS
money for nothing

M2

Wise Publications
London/New York/Sydney/Cologne

Exclusive distributors:
Music Sales Limited
8/9 Frith Street. London W1V 5TZ, England.

Music Sales Pty Limited
120 Rothschild Avenue, Rosebery, NSW 2018, Australia.

This book © Copyright 1988 by Wise Publications
ISBN 0.7119.1681.0 Order No. AM72786

Book design by Mike Bell

Photo credits: Inside Front Cover; Deborah Feingold,
P5; Bob Mazzer, P7; Ebet Roberts, P8/9; Ebet Roberts/Brian Aris/
Bob Mazzer, P13; Didi Zill, P14/15; Didi Zill/Bob Mazzer/
Others Unknown, P17; Didi Zill, P19; Bob Mazzer,
P20/21; Unknown, Inside Back Cover; Unknown.

Music Sales' complete catalogue lists thousands of
titles and is free from your local music shop, or direct from
Music Sales Limited. Please send £1 in stamps for postage to
Music Sales Limited, 8/9 Frith Street, London W1V 5TZ.

Printed in the United Kingdom by
Loader Jackson Printers Limited, Arlesey, Bedfordshire.

Sultans Of Swing

February 1978

You get a shiver in the dark
It's raining in the park but meantime
South of the river you stop and you hold everything
A band is blowing Dixie double four time
You feel alright when you hear that music ring

You step inside but you don't see too many faces
Coming in out of the rain to hear the jazz go down
Too much competition too many other places
But not too many horns can make that sound
Way on downsouth way on downsouth London town

You check out Guitar George he knows all the chords
Mind he's strictly rhythm he doesn't want to make it cry or sing
And an old guitar is all he can afford
When he gets up under the lights to play his thing

And Harry doesn't mind if he doesn't make the scene
He's got a daytime job he's doing alright
He can play honky tonk just like anything
Saving it up for Friday night
With the Sultans with the Sultans of Swing

And a crowd of young boys they're fooling around in the corner
Drunk and dressed in their best brown baggies and their platform soles
They don't give a damn about any trumpet playing band
It ain't what they call rock and roll
And the Sultans played Creole

And then the man he steps right up to the microphone
And says at last just as the time bell rings
'Thank you goodnight now it's time to go home'
And he make it fast with one more thing
'We are the Sultans of Swing'

Down To The Waterline

February 1978

Sweet surrender on the quayside
You remember we used to run and hide
In the shadow of the cargoes I take you one time
And we're counting all the numbers down to the waterline

Near misses on the dogleap stairways
French kisses in the darkened doorways
A foghorn blowing out wild and cold
A policeman shines a light upon my shoulder

Up comes a coaster fast and silent in the night
Over my shoulder all you can see are the pilot lights
No money in our jackets and our jeans are torn
Your hands are cold but your lips are warm

She can see him on the jetty where they used to go
She can feel him in the places where the sailors go
When she's walking by the river and the railway line
She can still hear him whisper
Let's go down to the waterline

Portobello Belle
June 1983

Belladonna's on the high street
Her breasts upon the offbeat
And the stalls are just the side shows
Victoriana's old clothes
Yeah she got the skirt so tight now
She wanna travel light now
She wanna tear up all her roots now
She got the turn-up on the boots now
She thinks she's tough
She ain't no English rose
But the blind singer
He's seen enough and he knows
He do a song about a long-gone Irish girl
But I got one for you my Portobello Belle

She sees a man upon his back there
Escaping from a sack there
And Belladonna lingers
Her gloves they got no fingers
Blind man he's singing the Irish
He get his money in a tin dish
Just a corner serenader
Once upon a time he could have made her
She thinks she's tough
She ain't no English rose
But the blind singer
He's seen enough and he knows
He do a song about a long-gone Irish girl
But I got one for you my Portobello Belle

Yes and these barrow boys are hawking
And a parakeet is squawking
Upon a truck a paper rhino
She get the crying of a wino
And then she get the reggae rumble
Belladonna's in the jungle
But she ain't no garden flower
There ain't no distress in the tower
Belladonna walks
Belladonna taking control
She don't care about your window box
Or your button hole
She sing a song about a long-gone Irish girl
But I got one for you my Portobello Belle

Twisting By The Pool
October 1982

We're going on a holiday now
Gonna take a villa, a small chalet
On the Costa del Magnifico
Where the cost of living is so low
Yeah, we're gonna be so neat
Dance to the Eurobeat
Yeah, we're gonna be so cool
Twisting by the pool

Sitting in a small café now
Swing, swing, swinging to the cabaret
You wanna see a movie, take in a show now
Meet new people at the disco
Yeah, we're gonna be so neat
Dance to the Eurobeat
Yeah, we're gonna be so cool
Twisting by the pool

And we can still get information
Reading all about inflation
And you're never gonna be out of reach
There's a call-box on the beach

Mmm, you're gonna look so cute
Sunglasses and a bathing suit
Be the baby of my dreams
Like the ladies in the magazines
Yeah, we're gonna be so neat
Dance to the Eurobeat
Oh yeah, we're gonna be so cool
Twisting by the pool

I'm a twisting fool
Just twisting, yeah, twisting
Twisting by the pool

Tunnel Of Love

July 1980

Getting crazy on the waltzers but it's the life that I choose
Sing about the sixblade sing about the switchback and a torture tattoo
And I been riding on a ghost train where the cars they scream and slam
And I don't know where I'll be tonight but I'd always tell you where I am

In a screaming ring of faces I seen her standing in the light
She had a ticket for the races just like me she was a victim of the night
I put my hand upon the lever said let it rock and let it roll
I had the one arm bandit fever there was an arrow through my heart and my soul

And the big wheel keep on turning neon burning up above
And I'm just high on the world
Come on and take a low ride with me girl
On the tunnel of love

It's just the danger when you're riding at your own risk
She said you are the perfect stranger she said baby let's keep it like this
It's just a cakewalk twisting baby step right up and say
Hey mister give me two give me two cos two can play

And the big wheel keep on turning neon burning up above
And I'm just high on the world
Come on and take the low ride with me girl
On the tunnel of love

Well it's been money for muscle another whirligig
Money for muscle another girl I dig
Another hustle just to make it big
And rockaway rockaway

And girl it looks so pretty to me just like it always did
Like the Spanish City to me when we were kids
Oh girl it looks so pretty to me just like it always did
Like the Spanish City to me when we were kids

She took off a silver locket she said remember me by this
She put her hand in my pocket I got a keepsake and a kiss
And in the roar of dust and diesel I stood and watched her walk away
I could have caught up with her easy enough
But something must have made me stay

And the big wheel keep on turning neon burning up above
And I'm just high on the world
Come on and take a low ride with me girl
On the tunnel of love

And now I'm searching through these carousels and the carnival arcades
Searching everywhere from steeplechase to palisades
In any shooting gallery where promises are made
To rockaway rockaway from Cullercoats and Whitley Bay out to rockaway

And girl it looks so pretty to me like it always did
Like the Spanish City to me when we were kids
Girl it looks so pretty to me like it always did
Like the Spanish City to me when we were kids

Romeo And Juliet

July 1980

A lovestruck Romeo sings a streetsuss serenade
Laying everybody low with a lovesong that he made
Finds a convenient streetlight steps out of the shade
Says something like you and me babe how about it?

Juliet says hey it's Romeo you nearly gimme a heart attack
He's underneath the window she's singing hey la my boyfriend's back
You shouldn't come around here singing up at people like that
Anyway what you gonna do about it?

Juliet the dice were loaded from the start
And I bet and you exploded in my heart
And I forget I forget the movie song
When you gonna realise it was just that the time was wrong Juliet?

Come up on different streets they both were streets of shame
Both dirty both mean yes and the dream was just the same
And I dreamed your dream for you and now your dream is real
How can you look at me as if I was just another one of your deals?

When you can fall for chains of silver you can fall for chains of gold
You can fall for pretty strangers and the promises they hold
You promised me everything you promised me thick and thin
Now you just say oh Romeo yeah you know I used to have a scene with him

Juliet when we made love you used to cry
You said I love you like the stars above I'll love you till I die
There's a place for us you know the movie song
When you gonna realise it was just that the time was wrong Juliet?

I can't do the talk like they talk on TV
And I can't do a love song like the way it's meant to be
I can't do everything but I'd do anything for you
I can't do anything except be in love with you

And all I do is miss you and the way we used to be
All I do is keep the beat and bad company
All I do is kiss you through the bars of a rhyme
Julie I'd do the stars with you any time

Juliet when we made love you used to cry
You said I love you like the stars above I'll love you till I die
And there's a place for us you know the movie song
When you gonna realise it was just that the time was wrong Juliet?

A lovestruck Romeo sings a streetsuss serenade
Laying everybody low with a lovesong that he made
Finds a convenient streetlight steps out of the shade
Says something like you and me babe how about it?

Where Do You Think You're Going?

November 1978

Where do you think you're going?
Don't you know it's dark outside?
Where do you think you're going?
Don't you care about my pride?
Where do you think you're going?
I think you don't know
You got no way of knowing
There's really no place you can go

I understand your changes
Long before you reach the door
I know where you think you're going
I know what you came here for
And now I'm sick of joking
You know I like you to be free
Where do you think you're going?
I think you better go with me girl

You say there is no reason
But you still find cause to doubt me
If you ain't with me girl
You're gonna be without me

Where do you think you're going?
Don't you know it's dark outside?
Where do you think you're going?
I wish I didn't care about my pride
And now I'm sick of joking
You know I like you to be free
So where do you think you're going?
I think you better go with me girl

Walk Of Life

December 1984

Here comes Johnny singing oldies, goldies
Be-Bop-A-Lula, Baby What I Say
Here comes Johnny singing I Gotta Woman
Down in the tunnels, trying to make it pay
He got the action, he got the motion
Yeah the boy can play
Dedication devotion
Turning all the night time into the day

He do the song about the sweet lovin' woman
He do the song about the knife
He do the walk, he do the walk of life

Here comes Johnny and he'll tell you the story
Hand me down my walkin' shoes
Here come Johnny with the power and the glory
Backbeat the talkin' blues
He got the action, he got the motion
Yeah the boy can play
Dedication devotion
Turning all the night time into the day

He do the song about the sweet lovin' woman
He do the song about the knife
He do the walk, he do the walk of life

Here comes Johnny singing oldies, goldies
Be-Bop-A-Lula, Baby What I Say
Here comes Johnny singing I Gotta Woman
Down in the tunnels, trying to make it pay
He got the action, he got the motion
Yeah the boy can play
Dedication devotion
Turning all the night time into the day

And after all the violence and double talk
There's just a song in all the trouble and the strife
You do the walk, you do the walk of life

Private Investigations
May 1982

It's a mystery to me — the game commences
For the usual fee — plus expenses
Confidential information — it's in a diary
This is my investigation — it's not a public inquiry

I go checking out the reports — digging up the dirt
You get to meet all sorts in this line of work
Treachery and treason — there's always an excuse for it
And when I find the reason I still can't get used to it

And what have you got at the end of the day?
What have you got to take away?
A bottle of whisky and a new set of lies
Blinds on the window and a pain behind the eyes

Scarred for life — no compensation
Private investigations

Telegraph Road
June 1983

A long time ago came a man on a track
Walking thirty miles with a sack on his back
And he put down his load where he thought it was best
And he made a home in the wilderness
He built a cabin and a winter store
And he ploughed up the ground by the cold lake shore
And the other travellers came riding down the track
And they never went further and they never went back
Then came the churches then came the schools
Then came the lawyers then came the rules
Then came the trains and the trucks with their loads
And the dirty old track was the telegraph road

Then came the mines — then came the ore
Then there was the hard times then there was a war
Telegraph sang a song about the world outside
Telegraph road got so deep and so wide
Like a rolling river...

And my radio says tonight it's gonna freeze
People driving home from the factories
There's six lanes of traffic
Three lanes moving slow...

I used to like to go to work but they shut it down
I've got a right to go to work but there's no work here to be found
Yes and they say we're gonna have to pay what's owed
We're gonna have to reap from some seed that's been sowed
And the birds up on the wires and the telegraph poles
They can always run away from this rain and this cold
You can hear them singing out their telegraph code
All the way down the telegraph road

You know I'd sooner forget but I remember those nights
When life was just a bet on a race between the lights
You had your head on my shoulder you had your hand in my hair
Now you act a little colder like you don't seem to care...
But believe in me baby and I'll take you away
From out of this darkness and into the day
From these rivers of headlights these rivers of rain
From the anger that lives on the streets with these names
'Cos I've run every red light on memory lane
I've seen desperation explode into flames
And I don't want to see it again...

From all of these signs saying sorry but we're closed
All the way down the telegraph road

Money For Nothing

December 1984

Now look at them yo-yo's that's the way you do it
You play the guitar on the MTV
That ain't workin' that's the way you do it
Money for nothin' and chicks for free
Now that ain't workin' that's the way you do it
Lemme tell ya them guys ain't dumb
Maybe get a blister on your little finger
Maybe get a blister on your thumb

We gotta install microwave ovens
Custom kitchen deliveries
We gotta move these refrigerators
We gotta move these colour TVs

See the little faggot with the earring and the make-up
Yeah buddy that's his own hair
That little faggot got his own jet airplane
That little faggot he's a millionaire

We gotta install microwave ovens
Custom kitchen deliveries
We gotta move these refrigerators
We gotta move these colour TVs

I shoulda learned to play the guitar
I shoulda learned to play them drums
Look at that mama, she got it stickin' in the camera
Man we could have some fun
And he's up there, what's that? Hawaiian noises?
Bangin' on the bongoes like a chimpanzee
That ain't workin' that's the way you do it
Get your money for nothin' get your chicks for free

We gotta install microwave ovens
Custom kitchen deliveries
We gotta move these refrigerators
We gotta move these colour TVs, Lord

Now that ain't workin' that's the way you do it
You play the guitar on the MTV
That ain't workin' that's the way you do it
Money for nothin' and your chicks for free
Money for nothin' and chicks for free

Brothers In Arms

December 1984

These mist covered mountains
Are a home now for me
But my home is the lowlands
And always will be
Some day you'll return to
Your valleys and your farms
And you'll no longer burn
To be brothers in arms

Through these fields of destruction
Baptisms of fire
I've watched all your suffering
As the battles raged higher
And though they did hurt me so bad
In the fear and alarm
You did not desert me
My brothers in arms

There's so many different worlds
So many different suns
And we have just one world
But we live in different ones

Now the sun's gone to hell
And the moon's riding high
Let me bid you farewell
Every man has to die
But it's written in the starlight
And every line on your palm
We're fools to make war
On our brothers in arms

Sultans Of Swing

Words & Music by Mark Knopfler

Additional Verses

3. You check out Guitar George, he knows all the chords.
    Mind he's strictly rhythm, he doesn't want to make it cry or sing.
    An old guitar is all he can afford,
      when he gets up under the lights, to play his thing.

4. And Harry doesn't mind if he doesn't make the scene.
    He's got a daytime job and he's doin' all right.
    He can play honky-tonk just like anything,
      savin' it up for Friday night
      with the Sultans, with the Sultans of swing.

5. And a crowd of young boys, they're foolin' around in the corner,
      drunk and dressed in their best brown baggies and their platform soles.
    They don't give a damn about any trumpet playin' band;
      it ain't what they call rock and roll.
    And the Sultans of swing played Creole.

6. *Instrumental*

7. And then The Man, he steps right up to the microphone
      and says, at last, just as the time-bell rings:
    "Thank you, good night, now it's time to go home."
    And he make it fast with one more thing:
    "We are the Sultans of Swing."

    (To Coda)

Down To The Waterline

Words & Music by Mark Knopfler

down to the wa - ter - line.____ Well,____

____ upon my shoul - der.

3. Up comes a coast - er, fast and si - lent in the night.____
4. see him on the jet - ty where they used to go. ____

O - ver my shoul - der, all you can see____ are the

She can feel____ him in the plac - es where the sail - ors go. ____

Portobello Belle

Words & Music by Mark Knopfler

side - shows,   vic - tor - i - an - a's   old   clothes.
lin - gers,   her gloves they got no   fin - gers.
rhi - no,   she get the cry - ing of a   wi - no.

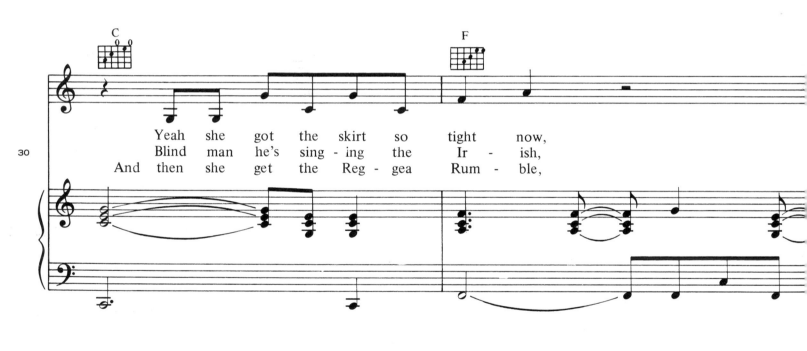

Yeah she got the skirt so   tight   now,
Blind man he's sing - ing the   Ir - ish,
And then she get the Reg - gea   Rum - ble,

she wan - na tra - vel light now,   she wan - na tear up all her
he get his mo - ney in a tin dish,   just a cor - ner ser - en
Bel - la - don - na's in the jun - gle,   but she ain't no gar - der

Twisting By The Pool

Words & Music by Mark Knopfler

33

Tunnel Of Love

Words & Music by Mark Knopfler

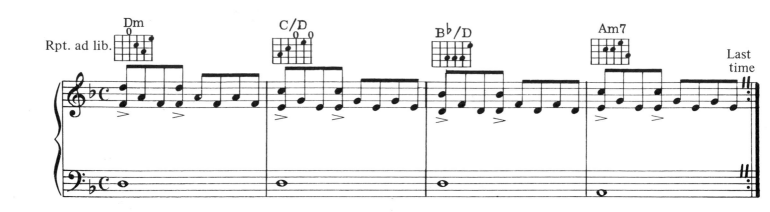

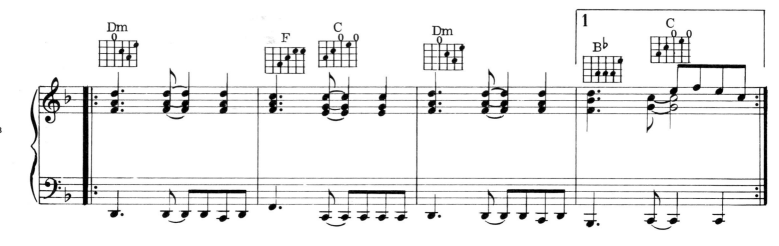

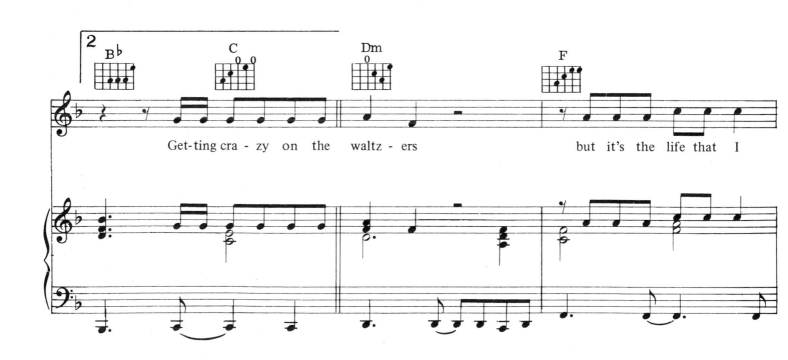

Get-ting cra - zy on the waltz - ers   but it's the life that I

41

low ride___ with me girl on the tun-nel of love.___

(See block lyric) It's just the

Well it's been mon-ey for mus-cle an-
(%) And now I'm search-ing through these car-ous-els and the

oth-er whir-li-gig Search-ing
car-ni-val arc-ades,___ ev-'ry-where___ from stee-ple-

45

(See block lyric) She took off a sil - ver

D.%. al Coda
(to 2nd bar)

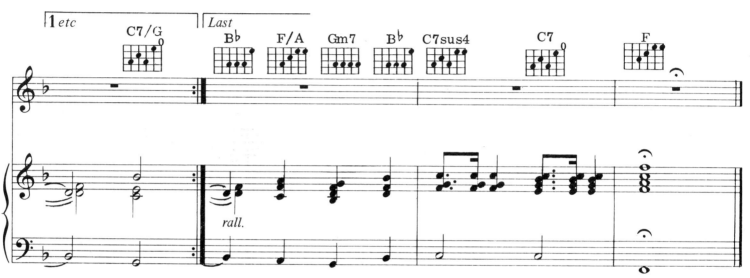

48

Additional Verses

It's just the danger,
When you're riding at your own risk.
She said you're the perfect stranger
She said baby let's keep it like this.
It's just a cake walk,
Twisting baby, step right up and say
Hey mister, give me two, give me two
'Cause two can play.

She took off a silver locket
She said remember me by this
She put her hand in my pocket
I got a keepsake and a kiss.
And in the roar of dust and diesel
I stood and watched her walk away
I could have caught up with her easy enough
But something must have made me stay.

Romeo And Juliet

Words & Music by Mark Knopfler

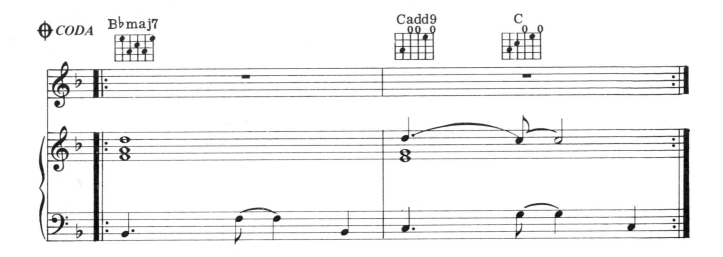

VERSE 2: Come up on different streets
They both were streets of shame.
Both dirty, both mean,
Yes and the dream was just the same.
And I dreamed your dream for you
And now your dream is real.
How can you look at me
As if I was just another one of your deals.

When you can fall for chains of silver
You can fall for chains of gold
You can fall for pretty strangers
And the promises they hold.
You promised me everything,
You promised me thick and thin
Now you just say oh Romeo, yeah,
You know I used to have a scene with him.

CHORUS 2: Juliet, when we made love you used to cry
You said I love you like the stars above,
I'll love you till I die.
There's a place for us
You know the movie song,
When you gonna realise
It was just that the time was wrong,
Juliet?

VERSE 3: I can't do the talk
Like they talk on T.V.
And I can't do a love song
Like the way it's meant to be.
I can't do everything
But I'd do anything for you
I can't do anything
Except be in love with you.

And all I do is miss you
And the way we used to be
All I do is keep the beat
And bad company.
All I do is kiss you
Through the bars of a rhyme
Julie I'd do the stars
With you any time.

CHORUS 3: Juliet, when we made love you used to cry
You said I love you like the stars above,
I'll love you till I die.
And there's a place for us
You know the movie song,
When you gonna realise
It was just that the time was wrong,
Juliet?

53

Where Do You Think You're Going?

Words & Music by Mark Knopfler

Moderately slow

(1. 3.) Where do you think you're go - ing,   don't you know it's dark out-side?
(2.) I un - der - stand your chan-ges,   long be - fore you reach the door,

Where do you think you're go - ing,   don't you care a - bout my pride?
I know where you think you're going   I know what you came here for.
(3.) I wish I did - n't care a - bout my pride.

To Coda ⊕

(1.) Where do you think you're go - ing? I think you don't know.
(2. 3.) and now I'm sick of joking you know I like you to be free.

You got no way of know-ing, there's real-ly no place you can go.
(3.) (So) Where do you think you're go - ing, I think you better go with me

girl.

Walk Of Life

Words & Music by Mark Knopfler

(1.& 𝄋) Here comes John - ny sing - ing
(2.) Here comes John - ny and he'll

yeah   the boy   can play___   de - di - ca - tion___
yeah   the boy   can play___   de - di - ca - tion___
yeah   the boy   can play___   de - di - ca - tion___

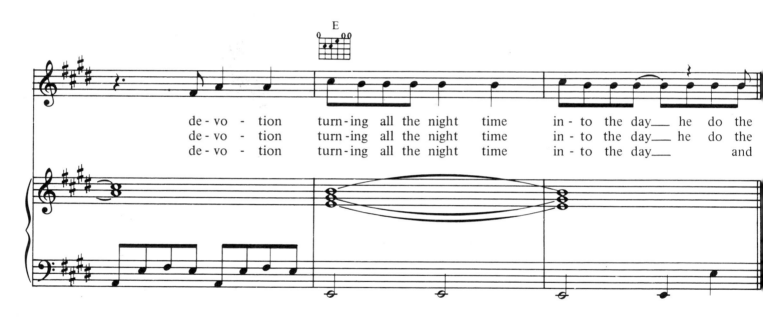

de - vo - tion   turn - ing all the night time   in - to the day___ he do the
de - vo - tion   turn - ing all the night time   in - to the day___ he do the
de - vo - tion   turn - ing all the night time   in - to the day___ and

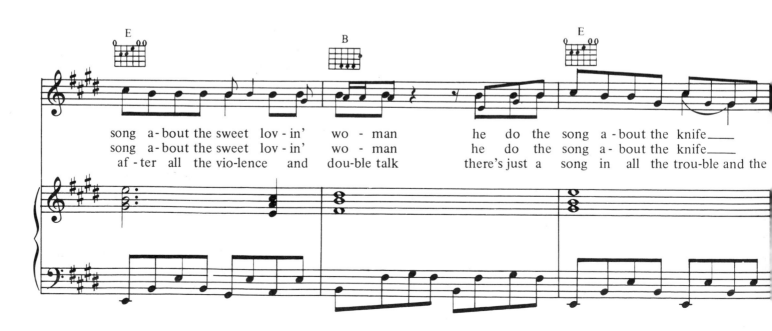

song a - bout the sweet lov - in' wo - man   he do the song a - bout the knife___
song a - bout the sweet lov - in' wo - man   he do the song a - bout the knife___
af - ter all the vio - lence and dou - ble talk   there's just a song in all the trou - ble and the

Private Investigations

Words & Music by Mark Knopfler

Telegraph Road

Words & Music by Mark Knopfler

2 x

Small notes 2nd time

A long time a - go___ came a man on a track___ walk-ing thir - ty miles with a
Then came the mines___ then came the ore___ then there was the hard times

73

Money For Nothing

Words & Music by Mark Knopfler & Sting

1. Now look at them yo - yo's   that's the way you do it
5.(%) I shoulda learned   to play the gui - tar
7.(%%) Now that ain't work - in'   that's the way to do it

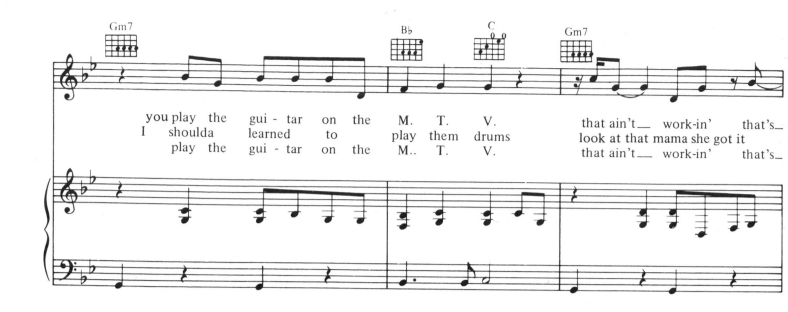

you play the gui - tar on the M. T. V.   that ain't __ work-in'   that's __
I shoulda learned to play them drums   look at that mama she got it
play the gui - tar on the M.. T. V.   that ain't __ work-in'   that's __

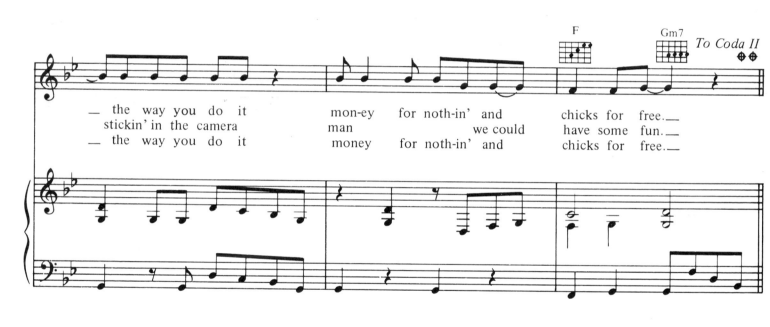

__ the way you do it   mon-ey for noth-in' and   chicks for free. __
stickin' in the camera   man   we could   have some fun. __
__ the way you do it   money for noth-in' and   chicks for free. __

To Coda II

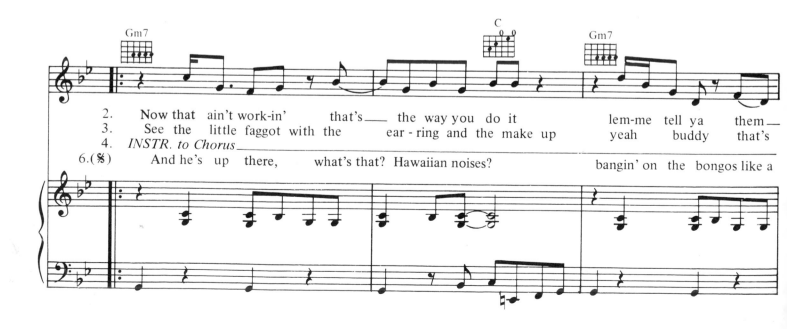

2. Now that ain't work-in'   that's __ the way you do it   lem-me tell ya them __
3. See the little faggot with the ear - ring and the make up   yeah buddy that's
4. INSTR. to Chorus _____
6.(𝄋) And he's up there, what's that? Hawaiian noises?   bangin' on the bongos like a

Brothers In Arms
Words & Music by Mark Knopfler

83

(Guitar solo)

86

There's so ma-ny diffe-rent worlds.   so ma-ny diffe-rent

suns   and we have just one   world

but we live in diffe-rent ones.

Guitar solo

Now the sun's gone to hell ___

Guitar solo
Ad lib. Guitar solo to FADE

Repeat to Fade